FAST AND FUN
FOLDED
CARDS™

EDITED BY **TANYA FOX**

Annie's Attic®

Fast and Fun Folded Cards

EDITOR Tanya Fox

MANAGING EDITOR Barb Sprunger

ART DIRECTOR Brad Snow

PUBLISHING SERVICES DIRECTOR Brenda Gallmeyer

ASSISTANT ART DIRECTOR Nick Pierce

COPY SUPERVISOR Michelle Beck

COPY EDITORS Amanda Ladig, Susanna Tobias

TECHNICAL EDITOR Brooke Smith

PHOTOGRAPHY SUPERVISOR Tammy Christian

PHOTOGRAPHY Matt Owen, Justin Wiard, Kelly Wiard

PHOTO STYLIST Tammy Steiner

GRAPHIC ARTS SUPERVISOR Ronda Bechinski

GRAPHIC ARTISTS Erin Augsburger, Pam Gregory

PRODUCTION ASSISTANTS Marj Morgan, Judy Neuenschwander

Printed in the United States of America
First Printing: 2008
ISBN: 978-1-59635-235-3

RETAIL STORES: If you would like to carry this book or any other DRG publications, visit DRGwholesale.com

Every effort has been made to ensure that the instructions in this publication are complete and accurate. We cannot, however, take responsibility for human error, typographical mistakes or variations in individual work. Please visit AnniesCustomerCare.com to check for pattern updates.

3 4 5 6 7 8 9

Contents

How rare and wonderful is that flash of a moment when we realize we have discovered a friend.
~ William E. Rothschild

If you're looking for creative and interesting ways to add pizzazz to your handmade cards, try adding a few extra folds to the design. I've always found folds are a great way to jazz up a basic card design, and adding folds doesn't require any expensive tools or supplies.

All you'll need is card stock, a measuring tool and a sharp cutting tool. A bone folder is a great tool for creating perfectly folded pieces, but a craft stick or your fingernail will be sufficient to get you started.

In this book, we'll explore fun ways to make gatefolds, accordion folds, tea bag folds and folds that you create using templates. Whether you choose to design a card with a center opening, one that includes multiple panels, or create a card with more dimension, I know you're going to enjoy this creative card-making journey. With just a little bit of practice, you'll soon be using these techniques and inspiring designs to create your own custom-made greeting cards.

Happy card making,

Accordion Folds

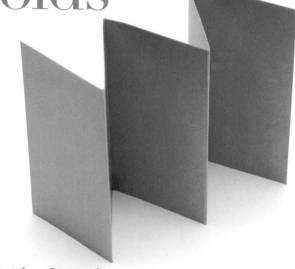

Like the musical instrument for which they are named, accordion cards are pleated—back-and-forth folds that create dimension and excitement. Picture a mountain range with valleys between the peaks. Accordion cards use terminology borrowed from the landscape. Folds that extend upward are called "mountain" folds, while those that dip down are "valley" folds.

Diagrams for accordion cards use two different kinds of dotted lines for the two kinds of folds, or two different colors—and it is important to get the mountain and valley folds in the right places.

With a simple card that is folded in half, the scoring and folding is important but not critical. You can always trim a bit if you're off-center. With accordion cards, however, take your time—careful measuring, scoring and folding spell the difference between a terrific accordion card and a lopsided disaster.

Proportion is a key element in accordion cards. If folds are close together, the effect is akin to a fan. The smaller the card, the closer the folds can be. For example, folds that are spaced at 1-inch intervals work fine for a gift tag, but panels on a traditional card are usually 2 to 4 inches wide.

Folds can be evenly or unevenly spaced, and accordion cards can fold from a center panel, forming pleated panels both left and right and/or heading in one direction (left to right) only.

All of the elements on an accordion card can be contained within the panels; or they can extend beyond the folds, peeking out when the card is closed, but often revealing more when the card is opened.

Getting Started

Because accordion cards often require long strips of card stock, you may need to glue pieces together. Measure and cut the strip to the dimensions required.

If you have a scoring board, use the ruler across the top to measure and position each score line. Flip the card stock, alternating right side up and right side down, as you score lines for mountain and valley folds.

For other scoring tools, measure carefully, and make light pencil marks for guidelines. A quilting ruler with a grid is helpful.

More Possibilities

By making additional cuts and folds to alter the shape and direction of the panels, you can give your accordion cards an entirely different look—a look with more complexity and dimension, but only a little bit more work. Turn accordion cards into flip-flop cards or Z-fold cards with these simple changes and additions. ✻

Gatefold Cards

Like double doors or divided gates, gatefold and fold-back cards invite you to open them and see what's inside.

Gatefold

The most common kind of gatefold card opens from the left and the right, with folds at the sides, the two flaps meeting in the middle. But there are no rules that the dividing line has to be in the center and that the flaps have to be the same size or can't overlap.

There are five possible flat surfaces to embellish: the two flaps (front and back of both of the side panels) and the center inside panel that you see as soon as the card is open. Most gatefold cards focus attention on the front flaps and center inside panel, leaving the inside of each flap a solid color, but those two extra inside panels offer space for decorative papers, text, stamping, pockets and more.

Remember, although gatefold cards are simple and easy to make, careful, accurate measuring and scoring are very important.

Tips & Ideas

To change the look of a card, choose a different color combination and vary the embellishments. A fold-back black tuxedo with black bow tie and white shirt can easily become a professorial plaid jacket with polka-dot bow tie. A man's Hawaiian shirt with a floral print can turn into a woman's blouse with a lacy patterned paper and trim at the collar and sleeves. Turn a fold-back Christmas tree into a Deco-inspired geometric triangle topped with half-circles and mini dots. Turn a flower-encrusted gatefold into a winter scene with snowflakes. ✹

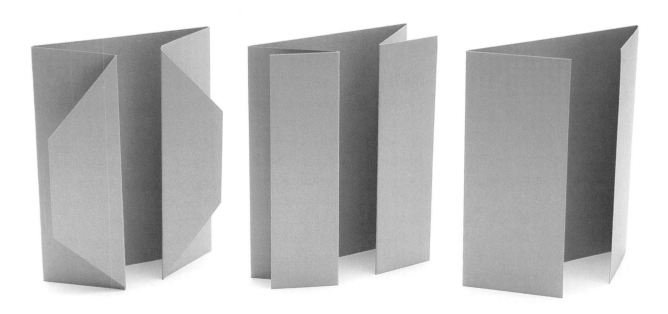

Cut N Fold

Templates from Hot Off The Press

Safety first: Always keep cutting tools away from children and pets, and take all necessary precautions to safeguard your eyes and hands.

With simple tools and a little time and patience, it's easy to add dimensional design elements to a card. You'll need paper or card stock, low-tack removable/reusable tape, a pencil, a cutting mat and a craft knife. You will also need a ruler or a cut-and-fold template. If this is your first attempt at making a cut-and-fold card, here are some helpful tips to keep in mind:

• Practice on inexpensive paper while you are learning the technique.

• Because each kind of paper or card stock cuts differently, it's also a good idea to buy some extra so you can practice on the "real thing" when you are making cards.

• Papers and card stocks with different patterns or colors on each side will produce impressive results. Experiment and have fun learning which papers work best for your project.

Templates

There are three kinds of cut-and-fold templates: plastic, metal and paper.

Durable plastic and metal templates have slits and dotted lines; each slit equals a cutting line, and each dotted line shows where to fold.

When using metal templates, the cuts are made while the template is taped in position; with plastic, the slits are used for drawing pencil guidelines, and cuts are made after the template is removed.

Paper templates, available via the internet or photocopied with permission from books and magazines, have solid lines for cutting and dotted lines for folds. These templates can be used only once because you cut through them in order to use them. Make extra copies, one for each card.

Tips

• Use a fresh blade as often as needed to make precise cuts.

• The key to cut-and-fold designs is making sure you have accurate, cleanly cut lines and careful folds. Take your time, and enjoy the process as well as the results.

Dies, Machines & Precut Card Stock

Cut-and-fold dies are a good way to create patterns without having to do any measuring or cutting by hand. Companies like POP-UPs from Plane Class sell ready-to-fold, precut card-stock pieces. Type the words "cut-and-fold patterns" into your favorite computer search engine and you will find free patterns as well as companies where you can shop for templates and tools. ✳

Tea Bag Folds

Tea bag folding starts with a simple square of lightweight paper, carefully and precisely folded. Individual folded squares are combined with other squares folded the same way. The resulting motif resembles a kaleidoscope, flower or geometric design that is flat enough to add to a card and send through the mail.

Tea bag folding, like origami, is portable, easy to learn, and requires little in the way of tools and supplies. Tea bag folded shapes, like flowers, can be simple or complex, incorporating just a few folded squares within a motif, or many. These motifs interlock and overlap—the possibilities are endless.

Choosing Papers

Choosing paper is a big part of the fun. Papers printed with squares, ready to cut apart, are a good way to start. These papers are available by the sheet or in books. You can also use rubber stamps or computer graphics to create your own. The key is using durable but lightweight papers that will hold nice, crisp folds. It's important to be able to repeat the same unit over and over so that the completed motifs have a precise elegance—very important to tea bag folding. Asian papers are the perfect weight and are usually high quality.

Getting Started

Select a paper with a simple pattern to practice making the folds. It may take a while before your fingers get the hang of it. Don't give up! If you were learning to play golf, you wouldn't think you had to be proficient after the first basket of balls, and tea bag folding is much easier than golf.

The tools are minimal: bone folder, craft knife, straight edge and cutting mat.

The supplies are equally minimal: paper and a pattern, a bit of glue or double-stick tape. If you buy precut papers, you don't even need the knife, ruler and mat. The bone folder is invaluable. Even if you have long fingernails, use the bone folder to get those crisp creases! It won't leave shiny marks on the paper the way your fingernails would.

Papers and stamps from Impression Obsession

Making Cards

Consider several tea bag folded motifs scattered on a card front like snowflakes—or lined up like flowers, with stems made of wire or ribbon. Add a single motif to a card-stock square. Layer the motif onto a card front. Simple or complicated, jazzy or serene, tea bag folding and the cards you'll make with the motifs you've created offer a lifetime of possibilities. ✸

Celebrating You

DESIGN BY **MICHELE BOYER**

Project note: *Use gray ink unless otherwise directed.*

1 Cut a 12 x 4-inch piece of gray card stock. With long side horizontal, score vertical lines 4 and 8 inches from left end. Set aside.

First panel: Stamp flowers three times without reinking onto a 2¼ x 3¼-inch piece of ivory card stock. Distress and ink edges. Adhere to a 3¾ x 3¾-inch piece of printed paper at an angle. Straight stitch along edges of stamped rectangle. Zigzag stitch diagonally across upper right corner of flowers rectangle.

2 Use black ink to stamp "BIRTHDAY WISHES" on ivory card stock; cut out and ink edges. Adhere across bottom of flowers rectangle as show in photo. Straight stitch across left end of sentiment; zigzag stitch along right end.

3 Fold a 3-inch length of ribbon in half; center unfolded ends on back of right side of square along edge forming a loop; straight stitch unfolded ends to square. Adhere one end of a 10-inch length of ribbon to back of square centered at left edge. Zigzag stitch along left side of square securing ribbon.

4 Distress edges of square. Punch a 1⁄16-inch hole through upper right and lower right corners; insert brads. Adhere to front card panel.

Second panel: Stamp flowers three times without reinking onto a 1¾ x 3-inch piece of ivory card stock; distress and ink edges. Adhere to right side of a 3¾ x 3¾-inch piece of printed paper. Straight stitch and zigzag stitch around edges of flowers rectangle.

5 Use black ink to stamp "inspire," "delight" and "grow" on ivory card stock; cut out and ink edges. Adhere to left side of paper square. Zigzag stitch along left edge of each word; straight stitch along right edge of each word. Straight stitch along left edge of printed paper square; distress edges. Use a brad to attach a photo turn to square next to upper left corner of flowers rectangle. Adhere to center panel.

Third panel: Stamp a flourish in upper right corner of a 3 x 3-inch piece of ivory card stock. Distress and ink edges. Attach two brads to upper left corner of square.

6 Use black ink to stamp "CELEBRATING YOU" on ivory card stock; cut out and ink edges. Adhere to

Materials
Card stock: gray, ivory
Provence 6 x 6-inch printed papers
Stamp sets: Nature Silhouettes,
   Beautiful, Essential Classic
   Expressions, Everyday Petites
Dye ink pads: gray, black
4 pewter brads
Pewter photo turn
20 inches ½-inch-wide ivory satin ribbon
Distressing tool
1⁄16-inch hole punch
Sewing machine with white thread
Paper adhesive

lower right area of ivory square. Zigzag stitch along left end of sentiment. Adhere ivory square to right side of a 3¾ x 3¾-inch piece of printed paper; distress edges.

7 Center one end of a 6½-inch length of ribbon on back of square letting ribbon extend from right side. Straight stitch around ivory square, stitching over ribbon end. Zigzag stitch along right end of "CELEBRATING YOU" sentiment. Adhere to right-hand panel.

8 Accordion fold scored lines. To close, insert one ribbon end through loop on first panel and tie ribbons into a bow. ✸

Sources: Card stock from Prism Papers; printed papers from Memory Box; rubber stamps from Cornish Heritage Farms; pewter brads and photo turn from We R Memory Keepers.

Birthday Surprise

DESIGN BY **KIMBER MCGRAY**

1 For accordion center, cut a 4¼ x 7-inch piece of Burst paper. With long side horizontal, score vertical lines every ½ inch beginning 1 inch from left end and stopping 1 inch from right end. Accordion fold scored lines.

2 For card front and back, cut two 4⅞ x 4-inch rectangles from Glee paper; round top corners on both pieces. Cut two 4½ x 3¾-inch rectangles from Burst paper; round top corners.

3 To assemble card, place Glee rectangles on worktable with circle sides facedown. Sandwich and adhere 1-inch end of accordion center between Burst rectangle and Glee rectangle, aligning straight edges with Burst rectangle blue side faceup. Repeat to attach other end of accordion center to other Glee rectangle.

4 Punch a 1½-inch circle from Crazy paper and a 2-inch scallop circle from Glee paper; adhere Crazy circle, red side faceup, to grid side of Glee circle. Punch a ⅟₁₆-inch hole through center of circle; attach "WISH" snap. Center and adhere ribbon to back of card, allowing ends to extend past edges.

5 Cut out several candles from printed paper and adhere to accordion folds inside card along with chipboard number. Cut two strips from "surprise!" section of printed paper to fit across card; adhere inside card, covering end of snap. Stamp "birthday" at bottom inside card with black ink; stamp "happy" above "birthday" with red ink.

Materials

White Out Frenzy double-sided printed card stock: Glee, Burst, Crazy
Surprise Scrap Strip printed paper
Stamps: "happy," "birthday"
Dye ink pads: red, black
Chipboard number
15 inches ⅜-inch-wide blue grosgrain ribbon
"WISH" snap
Punches: 1½-inch circle, 2-inch scallop circle, ⅟₁₆-inch hole, corner rounder
Paper adhesive

6 To close, wrap ribbon ends around to front, sliding ribbon underneath scallop circle and tie a knot. ✻

Sources: Printed card stock, ribbon and snap from We R Memory Keepers; printed paper from Scenic Route Paper Co.; chipboard number from Provo Craft; stamps from Unity Stamp Co.; punches from Uchida of America and EK Success.

He Loves Me

DESIGN BY **NIKI MEINERS**

1 Adhere Long Wing paper to both chipboard flowers; trim edges even. If desired, sand edges for a smooth finish.

2 Cut a 12 x 4¾-inch piece of pink card stock; score vertical lines every 4 inches, forming three panels. Accordion fold scored lines, folding first fold to the left.

3 Cut two 3¾ x 4½-inch rectangles from Monarch paper; adhere to first and third panels with striped side faceup. Stamp polka-dot ribbon on white card stock with pink ink; cut out and adhere to first panel ⅝ inch above bottom edge.

4 Punch three scallop ovals from chipboard; apply pink chalk ink to each oval. Ink edges red. Adhere one toward center bottom of each panel.

5 Adhere one chipboard flower to first panel. Cut off a three-petal section and one single petal from second flower. Adhere three-petal section to second panel; adhere single petal to third panel.

6 Thread a piece of fiber through each button; knot fibers on top of buttons and trim fiber ends. Apply a dot of glue to each knot; let dry. Adhere buttons to centers of flower petals on each panel.

7 Apply rub-on transfers to white card stock; cut a rectangle around each phrase. Ink edges red and adhere one to each scallop oval. Adhere a pearl to right end of each phrase. Add stickers as desired. Ink card edges red. ✶

Sources: Card stock from Prism Papers; printed papers, pearls and rub-on transfers from Kaisercraft; stamp set from Unity Stamp Co.; chalk ink pads from Clearsnap Inc.; chipboard flowers and stickers from Frances Meyer Inc.; scallop oval punch from Uchida of America; Zip Dry Paper Glue from Beacon Adhesives Inc.

Materials
Card stock: white, pink
Flutterby double-sided printed papers: Monarch, Long Wing
Chipboard
It's Spring! stamp set
Chalk ink pads: red, pink
2 chipboard flowers
Heart stickers
3 pink buttons
Red fiber
Rub-on transfers: 2 "He loves me," 1 "He loves me not"
3 red flat-back pearls
Sandpaper (optional)
Scallop oval punch
Instant-dry paper glue

Hello Pumpkin

DESIGN BY **LISA SILVER**

1 Cut a 10 x 5-inch piece of Gazebo paper; score vertical lines every 2 inches along length of paper. Cut down 3 inches along scored line on last panel; cut off top 2½ inches from last panel. Fold down top ½ inch on remainder of last panel and fold over to fourth panel; adhere bottom and side edges in place forming a pocket.

2 Cut a piece of Garden Path paper to fit second panel; adhere to second panel. Trim edges even. Accordion fold scored lines. Use template and cutting tool to cut a half-oval shape at top of folded card. *Note: If tool does not go through all layers, use scissors to complete cut.*

3 Attach an eyelet to center top of each panel, making sure holes align. Stamp desired images on first and third panels; color. Cut a small piece of orange card stock to fit inside pocket; stamp "hello pumpkin" on card stock with orange ink and insert inside pocket.

4 Close card. Cut a 1¼ x 2½-inch piece of Garden Path paper; round left corners and adhere to right side of front panel, aligning straight edges. Stamp "autumn" and a leaf on grid side of Gazebo paper with brown ink; cut a rectangle around words and ink edges brown. Adhere to front panel.

5 Thread brown ribbon through holes; wrap pink ribbon around brown ribbon and tie a bow. Trim ribbon ends as desired. ✽

Sources: Card stock from Prism Papers; printed papers from October Afternoon; stamp set from Cornish Heritage Farms; nylon ribbon from EK Success; jumbo eyelets from We R Memory Keepers; Coluzzle cutting template and cutting tool from Provo Craft; Zip Dry Paper Glue from Beacon Adhesives Inc.

Materials

Orange card stock
Detours double-sided printed papers:
  Gazebo, Garden Path
Fall Silhouettes stamp set
Dye ink pads: orange, brown
Colored pencils
Ribbon: 12 inches ⅝-inch-wide brown
  grosgrain, 6 inches ⅜-inch-wide peach
  nylon ribbon
4 jumbo eyelets with eyelet setter
Rounded tag template with cutting tool
Corner rounder
Instant-dry paper glue

Thinking of You

DESIGN BY **DIANE TUGGLE**

Project notes: *Ink edges as desired. Use paper adhesive unless otherwise directed.*

1 Begin with a 12 x 5½-inch piece of yellow card stock; score every ¾ inch along length. This will be center section of card.

2 Cut two 8½ x 5½-inch pieces of yellow card stock; fold each in half, forming two 4¼ x 5½-inch panels. Insert one ¾-inch end of accordion-folded center section inside one yellow panel; adhere in place. The end section should be sandwiched inside yellow

panel. Repeat to adhere opposite end of center section to other yellow panel.

3 Cut 18 3 x 1½-inch rectangles from yellow card stock. These will be tabs for letters inside card. Using double-sided tape, attach three tabs to each fold inside card, attaching top and bottom rows to right side of folds and middle row to left side of folds.

4 Cut 18 1¼ x 1¼-inch squares from white card stock. Stamp a letter on each square to spell "hope you are better." Ink edges of each square. Adhere letters to inside tabs, adhering letters on top and bottom rows to right side of folds and letters on middle row to left side of folds. Decorate blank tabs with stickers.

5 Adhere a 27-inch length of ribbon to center on card front, allowing 9 inches to extend past right edge. Center and adhere a 4 x 5¼-inch piece of green polka-dot paper to card front. Cut two 4-inch lengths of scallop border sticker; attach to top and bottom of polka-dot rectangle. Adhere a 2⅞ x 3⅜-inch floral rectangle to upper left area of polka-dot rectangle.

6 Stamp "THINKING OF YOU" on a 1½ x ¾-inch piece of yellow card stock; adhere to brown card stock and trim a small border. Adhere to upper left corner of floral rectangle. Attach a ¾-inch piece of scallop border sticker next to right end of words rectangle.

Materials

Card stock: yellow, brown, white
Perfect Day paper pack
Perfect Day stickers
Stamp sets: Thoughtful Seasons, small alphabet
Acrylic blocks
Brown dye ink pad
40 inches ⅝-inch-wide cream organdy ribbon
Small cream button
Sanding block
2¼-inch scallop square punch
Adhesive foam dots
Double-sided tape
Paper adhesive

7 Attach a flower sticker to yellow card stock; trim a narrow border. Punch a 2¼-inch scallop square from brown card stock; sand edges. Adhere flower sticker to scallop square. Adhere button to lower right corner. Adhere to lower right corner of card front with foam dots.

8 Cut three 3-inch lengths of ribbon. Knot center of each and trim ribbon ends as desired; adhere to upper left area of card front as shown.

9 Decorate inside panels as desired. ✳

Source: Card stock, paper pack, stickers, stamp sets, acrylic blocks, ink pads, button, ribbon, scallop punch, sanding block and foam dots from Close To My Heart.

With Gratitude

DESIGN BY **MELONY BRADLEY**

Project note: *Use black ink to stamp images; use brown ink to ink edges of papers as desired.*

1 Cut a 12 x 5½-inch piece of kraft card stock. With long side horizontal, score vertical lines 5, 5½, 6, 6½ and 7 inches from left end. Beginning with a valley fold, accordion fold scored lines to create accordion center. This should form a 5 x 5½-inch card.

Materials

Card stock: kraft, light blue
Printed papers: ivory with red dots, ivory with light brown dots, red
Stamps: Patterned Bugs set, "WITH Gratitude," "Thank YOU Very MUCH!"
Ink pads: black pigment, brown chalk
Black paper flower
Blue rhinestone brad
⅜-inch-wide ribbon: 3 inches light blue velvet, 20 inches red gingham
Punches: 2½-inch scallop circle, 1½-inch scallop circle, 2-inch flower, 2-inch circle, corner rounder
Instant-dry paper glue

Cut a 4¾ x 4-inch piece of red printed paper, a 4 x 3-inch piece of ivory with light brown dots paper, a 5 x ½-inch strip of ivory with red dots paper and a 5 x ¾-inch strip of light blue card stock. Cut a 5-inch length of red gingham ribbon; cut off left end at an angle. Round upper left corner of ivory polka-dot piece. Referring to photo for placement, adhere all pieces to card front. Stamp "WITH Gratitude" on light blue strip.

Punch 3-inch scallop circles from light blue card stock and red printed paper; punch a 2-inch circle from center of red scallop circle, creating a scallop frame. Stamp a dragonfly centered on light blue circle. Adhere red frame on top of light blue circle, aligning edges. Adhere to card front as shown.

Attach rhinestone brad to flower center. Cut velvet ribbon into two 1½-inch pieces; cut off one end on each at an angle. Adhere ribbons and flower to card front as shown.

Cut two 4¾ x 5¼-inch rectangles from ivory with red dots paper; adhere to inside panels. Stamp a row of ants vertically on right panel.

Punch a 1½-inch scallop circle from light blue card stock; stamp a beetle on circle. Punch a flower from red printed paper. Adhere beetle circle to flower. Stamp "Thank YOU" and "Very MUCH!" on light blue card stock. Cut out words. Adhere flower and word rectangles to center folds inside card.

Cut six small pieces of red gingham ribbon; trim one end of each at an angle. Adhere straight ends to center folds inside card. ✸

Sources: Printed papers from Making Memories and K&Company; stamp set from Inkadinkado; sentiment stamps from Anna Griffin Inc.; paper flower from Prima Marketing Inc.; punches from Uchida of America; Zip Dry Paper Glue from Beacon Adhesives Inc.

Baby Congrats

DESIGN BY **KIMBER MCGRAY**

Materials
Gold/ivory double-sided
 card stock
Jack Die Cut Stars printed paper
Animal Crackers Jack Border & Tag
 stickers
Green letter stickers
2 inches ⅜-inch-wide blue stitched
 ribbon
Black fine-tip pen
Adhesive foam square
Paper adhesive

Project note: For double-sided card stock, the color given in the instructions will be the front of the project.

1 Cut an 11 x 4¼-inch piece of gold card stock; with long side horizontal, score vertical lines 2¾ and 5½ inches from left end. Accordion fold scored lines making first fold a mountain fold.

2 Cut an 8¼ x 4¼-inch piece of printed paper; with long side horizontal, score a line 2¾ inches from left end. Adhere to inside panels of card, aligning folds.

3 Cut a 4¼-inch length of striped border sticker and attach to left edge of front panel. Attach giraffe sticker to ivory card stock; trim a narrow border. Adhere to right side of front panel as shown.

4 Cut a medium star and a tiny star from printed paper; adhere tiny star to medium star with foam square. Adhere to front panel as shown. Attach letter stickers to front panel to spell "congrats" replacing the letter "a" with stars.

5 Knot center of ribbon; trim ribbon ends at an angle and adhere to giraffe's neck. Attach "little one" sticker to large inside panel. Hand-write "welcome to this world," on sticker with black pen. ❋

Sources: Card stock from WorldWin Papers; printed paper and Animal Cracker stickers from Making Memories; letter stickers from Doodlebug Design Inc.; ribbon from American Crafts Inc.

Sisters

DESIGN BY **BARBARA HOUSNER**

Project note: Ink edges of papers as desired.

1 Cut an 11 x 4¼-inch piece of light tan card stock; with long side horizontal, score vertical lines 2¾ and 5½ inches from left end. Accordion fold scored lines making first fold a mountain fold.

2 Cut a 5¼ x 4-inch piece and a 5⅜ x 4⅛-inch piece of Floral paper; with floral side faceup, adhere smaller rectangle to solid-color side of larger rectangle. Adhere to large inside panel.

3 Hand-print, or use a computer to generate, desired quotation on reverse side of Dots paper. Trim to 2½ x 4 inches; adhere to solid-color side of a 2⅝ x 4⅛-inch piece of Floral paper. Adhere to small inside panel.

4 With dotted side faceup, adhere a 2½ x 4-inch piece of Dots paper to solid-color side of a 2⅝ x 4⅛-inch piece of Floral paper; adhere to front panel. Cut a ⅞ x 4-inch strip of Floral paper; create a scallop border along left edge with border punch. Adhere a ⅜ x 4-inch strip of dark pink card stock behind holes with solid color faceup; adhere to front panel ¼ inch from left edge.

5 Trim die cut to 4 x 2½ inches; use an unthreaded sewing machine to pierce holes along top and bottom of die cut. Adhere to solid-color side of Dots paper and trim a small border. Adhere to front flap as shown. ✹

Sources: Card stock from Bazzill Basics Paper Inc.; Wild Asparagus printed papers and die cut from My Mind's Eye; punch from Fiskars.

Materials
Light tan card stock
Baby Girl double-sided printed
  papers: Floral, Dots
Wild Asparagus Sisters die cut
Dark pink ink pad
Brown fine-tip pen
Threading Water border punch
Sewing machine
Paper adhesive
Computer and printer (optional)

Best Wishes

DESIGN BY **CARLA SCHAUER**

4 Ink edges of chipboard heart brown. Adhere to pink rectangle as shown. Stamp "Best Wishes" on a 2½ x ¾-inch piece of pink distressed paper with gray-green ink; ink edges pink and brown. Thread cream floss through each button and tie knots on top; trim floss ends. Adhere "Best Wishes" rectangle and buttons to heart as shown.

5 Adhere top half of assembled rectangle to top panel. Stamp "{love has no boundaries}" on pink distressed paper with turquoise ink; cut a 3 x 1½-inch rectangle around words. Distress and ink edges brown. Adhere to solid-color side of Fruitcake paper; trim a small border. Adhere inside card. ✱

Sources: Fruitcake printed paper from BasicGrey; Tea and Silk printed papers, chipboard heart and lace from Prima Marketing Inc.; Simple Sentiments stamp set from Technique Tuesday; Sentiments O' Simple stamp set from Unity Stamp Co.; ink pads from Clearsnap Inc.; Fabri-Tac Glue from Beacon Adhesives Inc.

Project note: *Use paper adhesive unless otherwise directed.*

1 Cut a 4¼ x 11-inch piece of light turquoise card stock; with short side horizontal, score horizontal lines 5½ and 8¼ inches from bottom edge. Accordion fold scored lines making first scored line a valley fold.

2 Adhere a 4¼ x 2¾-inch piece of green words paper to top panel; machine-stitch along edges of paper.

3 Cut a 2¾ x 4⅛-inch piece of Fruitcake paper; distress edges on solid-color side. Cut a 3¼ x 3⅛-inch piece of pink floral paper; crumple paper and then smooth out. Ink folds brown; ink edges pink. Adhere lace along right side of pink rectangle with fabric glue. Center and adhere to dark turquoise rectangle.

Materials

Light turquoise card stock
Fruitcake Glisten/Avalanche double-sided printed paper
Tea and Silk double-sided printed papers: pink floral, green words, pink distressed
Tea and Silk large chipboard heart
Stamp sets: Simple Sentiments, Sentiments O' Simple
Ink pads: pink chalk, brown chalk, gray-green dye, turquoise dye
3 inches green crocheted lace
Cream embroidery floss
Buttons: 1 turquoise, 1 pink, 1 ivory
Distressing tool
Sewing machine with cream thread
Fabric glue
Paper adhesive

How rare and wonderful is that flash of a moment when we realize we have discovered a friend.

~ William E. Rothschild

Rare & Wonderful

DESIGN BY **MICHELE BOYER**

1 Cut an 11 x 4¼-inch piece of brown card stock; with long side horizontal, score vertical lines 2¾ and 5½ inches from left end. Accordion fold scored lines making first fold a mountain fold.

2 Adhere a 2½ x 4-inch piece of printed paper to front panel. Use yellow ink to stamp geometric flowers onto a 5¼ x 4-inch piece of yellow card stock; ink edges brown. Use brown ink to stamp a flourish on upper right area of rectangle. Adhere to inside panel.

3 Stamp a sentiment onto ivory card stock with dark brown ink. Cut a rectangle around words and adhere to brown card stock; trim a narrow border. Adhere to right side of front panel as shown. Attach butterfly to lower right corner of yellow panel. To close, tuck corner of sentiment rectangle between layers of butterfly. ✳

Sources: Card stock from Prism Papers; Wild Saffron collection printed paper and butterfly sticker from K&Company; stamps from Cornish Heritage Farms.

Materials
Card stock: brown, yellow, ivory
Brown floral printed paper
Dimensional butterfly sticker
Stamps: Friend Centers set,
   Beautiful set, Geometric Flowers II
   Backgrounder
Dye ink pads: yellow, brown,
   dark brown
Paper adhesive

Welcome Neighbor

DESIGN BY **MICHELE BOYER**

Materials
Card stock: blue, white, orange
Meadow's Edge printed
  card-stock pack
A Welcome Hug stamp set
Black dye ink pad
Markers
Paper adhesive

centered on top of orange rectangle, but do not adhere. This will be the front of the card when card is closed.

4 Close card. Stamp a house centered on white card stock; stamp "Welcome" around house image on each side. Color house and adhere white rectangle to orange rectangle.

5 For inside of card, adhere a 3⅞ x 2⅞-inch piece of orange card stock to center panel. Stamp "To Our Neighborhood" at center top of a 3½ x 2⅝-inch piece of white card stock; stamp three houses centered below words. Color houses. Adhere to center panel. ✽

Sources: Card stock from Prism Papers; printed card stock from Rubber Soul; stamp set from Cornish Heritage Farms.

PATTERN ON PAGE 47

1 Cut a 6¾ x 5½-inch piece of blue card stock. Referring to pattern on page 47, score vertical lines as indicated by dashed lines; cut solid lines to create a center panel.

2 Cut pieces of orange printed card stock to fit left, right and top and bottom panels of card. Adhere in place as shown. Mountain fold first set of scored lines; valley fold last set of scored lines.

3 With card open, place it on worktable with printed card-stock side facedown. Adhere a 3⅞ x 2⅞-inch piece of orange card stock to center panel. Cut a 3½ x 2½-inch rectangle from white card stock; place

Fly Away

DESIGN BY **KIMBER MCGRAY**

Materials
Pink card stock
Happy double-sided printed papers:
    Flutter, Circles, Stripes
"fly away" stamp
Pink dye ink pad
½-inch circle punch
Sewing machine with white thread
Silver glitter glue
Paper adhesive

1 Cut an 8 x 4¼-inch piece of pink card stock; with long side horizontal, score vertical lines 2 and 4 inches from left end. Accordion fold scored lines, making first fold a mountain fold.

2 Cut a 5¾ x 3-inch piece of Stripes paper; with long side horizontal, score a vertical line 1¾ inches from left end. With yellow side faceup, adhere to inside panels, aligning folds. Machine-stitch along edges of Stripes paper.

3 Cut a 1⅞ x 4-inch piece of Circles paper. Punch seven ½-inch circles from Stripes paper. With green circles side of rectangle faceup, adhere striped circles to reverse side of rectangle along right edge to create a scallop border. Adhere to front panel; machine-stitch around edges of Circles paper.

4 Cut out a butterfly from Flutter paper; accent with glitter glue. Let dry. Adhere to front panel as shown applying adhesive to butterfly's body only. Stamp "fly away" on right side of inside panel. ✹

Sources: Card stock from WorldWin Papers; printed papers and stamp from Chatterbox Inc.

Hello

DESIGN BY **MICHELE BOYER**

1 Cut an 8½ x 5½-inch piece of olive green card stock; with long side horizontal, score and fold vertical lines 2⅛ inches from each end forming a 4¼ x 5½-inch gatefold card. Cut two 1⅞ x 5⅜-inch rectangles from printed paper; adhere one to left front flap floral side faceup.

2 Stamp two tree branches as shown on a 2⅝ x 3⅞-inch piece of white card stock; color. Stamp two birds on white card stock; color and cut out. Adhere to branches as shown. Add shading with gray marker.

3 Punch six flowers from printed paper; adhere to branches floral side faceup, leaving petals free of adhesive. Gently bend petals upward for dimension. Adhere rectangle to olive green card stock; trim a narrow border. Adhere rectangle to left front flap as shown.

4 Place plus and minus sides of magnetic snap together and remove adhesive from one half; adhere to reverse side of decorated panel. Remove adhesive from other half and close card. This half will adhere to right front flap. Open card, and adhere other printed rectangle to right front flap covering the magnetic half.

5 Stamp two branches on white card stock; color and cut out. Align branches with branches on

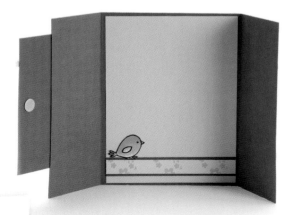

Materials

Card stock: olive green, ivory
Main Street double-sided printed paper
Stamp sets: The Landing Pad, Pretty
  Birds, Mocha Chica
Black dye ink pad
Markers
Tiny flower punch
Magnetic snap
Paper adhesive

card front; trim and adhere in place. Stamp "hello" on bottom of right front flap.

6 For inside, cut a 4 x 5⅜-inch piece of ivory card stock. Adhere to center panel inside card. Adhere a 4 x ½-inch strip of printed paper, floral side faceup, to a 4 x ⅝-inch strip of olive green card stock; adhere to ivory rectangle ¼ inch above bottom edge. Stamp a bird on white card stock; color and cut out. Adhere to lower left side of rectangle just above printed paper strip. ✱

Sources: Card stock from Prism Papers; printed paper from October Afternoon; stamp sets from Cornish Heritage Farms; tiny flower punch from McGill Inc.; magnetic snap from BasicGrey.

It's a Picnic

DESIGN BY **MELONY BRADLEY**

Project note: Ink edges of papers as desired with brown ink.

1. Cut a 10 x 6½-inch piece of argyle paper; with long side horizontal, score and fold vertical lines 2½ inches from each end, forming a 5 x 6½-inch gatefold card.

2. Cut one 4¼-inch circle from pink paper and one 4¼-inch circle from green paper. Cut a 3¼-inch circle from center of green circle, forming a ring. Cut pink circle and green ring in half. Adhere green ring to pink half-circle, forming a watermelon slice. Punch four ¹⁄₁₆-inch holes across top edge; insert brads.

3. Punch 1-inch circle from green paper. Apply rub-on transfers to spell "it's a" on green circle and "Picnic" on watermelon slice. Adhere circle to upper left side of watermelon slice; adhere to left front flap as shown.

4. Adhere a magnet strip to reverse side of watermelon slice; adhere other magnet strip to right front flap, adhering it so it aligns with first magnet.

5. Cut eight 2-inch and two 2½-inch lengths of ribbons; trim one end of each 2-inch ribbon at an

Materials
Green card stock
Coordinating printed papers: pink/green argyle, pink, green
Invitation information rubber stamps
Dye ink pads: brown, black
Black alphabet rub-on transfers
Various ⅜-inch-wide grosgrain ribbons to coordinate with printed papers
2 (¾-inch) magnet strips
4 black mini round brads
Punches: ¹⁄₁₆-inch hole, 1-inch circle
Instant-dry paper glue

angle. Referring to photo, adhere ribbons to upper left and lower right corners of card front.

6. Cut a 4¾ x 6-inch piece of green card stock; stamp invitation information on rectangle with black ink. Adhere inside card. ✳

Sources: Printed papers from Imaginisce; rub-on transfers from Making Memories and American Crafts Inc.; Zip Dry Paper Glue from Beacon Adhesives Inc.

It's the Little Things

DESIGN BY **NIKI MEINERS**

Materials

12 x 12-inch card stock: green, purple
Coordinating printed papers
Chipboard shapes: bird, frame, decorative panel
Stamp sets: Sentiments O'Simple, It's the Little Things
Ink pads: black dye, red dye, pink chalk
Paper flowers: 1 medium lavender, 1 small green, 1 mini burgundy
18 inches 1½-inch-wide red pucker ribbon
Large scallop-edge scissors
Fabric glue
Instant-dry paper glue

1 Cut one 12 x 6-inch piece and one 9 x 6-inch piece of green card stock. With long sides horizontal, score vertical lines 3 inches from each end on 12-inch piece and 3 inches from left end on 9-inch piece.

2 Fold flaps in toward center on 12-inch piece, forming a 6 x 6-inch gatefold card. Fold left flap to the right on 9-inch piece. Open pieces and adhere 3 x 6-inch left panel on 9-inch piece to right side of center panel of 12-inch piece, aligning folds.

3 Cut seven pieces of printed papers to fit front and inside panels. Cut an 8 x 4-inch piece of green card stock; with long side horizontal, score left, right and bottom sides 1 inch from edges. Trim top edge with scallop-edge scissors. Fold sides inward, forming a pocket; trim scallop sections to fit. Stamp "thanks" on upper right side of pocket with red ink. Apply pink ink to chipboard bird; adhere to left side of pocket. Adhere pocket to bottom on reverse side of center flap.

4 Cut a 4 x 2⅛-inch piece of purple card stock. Adhere to center bottom on front of center panel. Stamp "it's the little things…" on chipboard panel with black ink and adhere to purple rectangle.

5 Close card; wrap ribbon around card and tie a knot on right side. Remove ribbon. Apply pink ink to chipboard frame. Stamp "enjoy" on purple card stock with black ink; cut to fit inside frame. Adhere to back of frame. Adhere frame to ribbon next to knot. ***Note:*** *Do not glue both sides of ribbon together.* Let dry. Layer and adhere flowers to right side of frame. Slide ribbon onto card. Trim ribbon ends. ✳

Sources: Card stock from Prism Papers; printed papers from Scenic Route Paper Co.; flowers from Prima Marketing Inc.; chipboard bird from Colorbök; chipboard frame from Best Creation Inc.; chipboard panel from Autumn Leaves; stamp sets from Unity Stamp Co.; ink pads from Clearsnap Inc.; ribbon from The Ribbons House; Zip Dry Paper Glue and Fabri-Tac Glue from Beacon Adhesives Inc.

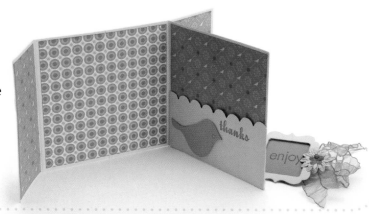

Thank You

DESIGN BY **KIMBER MCGRAY**

Materials

Card stock: light blue, white, White
    Out Frenzy Burst double-sided printed
Rubber stamps: Houndstooth
    Backgrounder, flowers, "Thank You"
Dye ink pads: red, black, light blue
3 blue mini round brads
Punches: 1/16-inch hole, 2-inch scallop
    circle, corner rounder
Adhesive foam dots
Paper adhesive

1 Cut a 10 x 5¼-inch piece of light blue card stock; with long side horizontal, score and fold vertical lines 2½ inches from each end to form a 5 x 5¼-inch gatefold card.

2 Cut two 2⅜ x 5-inch rectangles from white card stock; stamp houndstooth background on both with red ink. Adhere to front flaps.

3 Cut a 3¾ x 2½-inch piece of white card stock; round left-hand corners. Use black ink to stamp "Thank You" along bottom edge. Adhere to right front flap, aligning straight edges.

4 Punch a 2-inch scallop circle from printed card stock; adhere to upper right side of right front flap. Use red and light blue inks to stamp two flowers on white card stock; cut out. Punch three 1/16-inch holes through center of largest flower; insert brads. Layer and adhere flowers to right side of right front flap using foam dots. ❈

Sources: Card stock from WorldWin Papers; printed card stock from We R Memory Keepers; Houndstooth Backgrounder stamp from Cornish Heritage Farms; other stamps from Stampin' Up! and Stampabilities; punches from EK Success and Uchida of America.

Magic Moments

DESIGN BY **DIANE TUGGLE**

Project note: *Ink edges of papers as desired with distress ink.*

1 Cut a 12 x 5-inch piece of black card stock; with long side horizontal, score a vertical line 5 inches from left end; fold flap to the right. Adhere a 6½ x 4½-inch piece of polka-dot paper to inside right panel.

2 Cut a 12 x 4-inch piece of black card stock; with long side horizontal, score a vertical line 5½ inches from right end. Fold flap to the left. Adhere left flap to

right side of first piece as shown. This will form a trifold card; close left flap followed by right flap.

3 Open card. Adhere a 6 x 3½-inch piece of tan printed paper to center panel. Use light brown ink to stamp a circle on upper right corner. With black dye ink, stamp "CELEBRATE" on top of circle, "You only live once. Make it count." as shown.

4 Adhere a 4½ x 4½-inch piece of tan/black printed paper to left front flap. Stamp large clock face on

upper left corner with brown ink. Punch a 1¾-inch circle from white card stock; stamp the following on circle: "TIME" with black dye ink, a circle ring with brown ink and wavy lines with light brown ink. Adhere to left front flap overlapping clock face.

5 Cut a 4⅞ x 3½-inch rectangle from striped paper. Stamp a watch band on brown card stock; cut out and tear off one end. Adhere to rectangle as shown.

6 Die-cut a postage stamp from light brown card stock. Stamp "Congratulations Graduate" on die cut with black dye ink; stamp wavy lines over words with light brown ink. Adhere at an angle to upper left corner of rectangle.

7 Stamp clock face, numbers and clock hands on white card stock with black dye ink; cut out. Adhere to watch band as shown. Attach acrylic window on top of clock face. Punch a ¹⁄₁₆-inch hole next to right side of

Materials

Brown card stock
Silhouette Level 2 paper pack
   (includes card stock)
Stamp sets: Make It Count, Express
   Postage, Lovely Buckles
Acrylic blocks
Dye ink pads: brown, black, light brown
Black distress ink pad
Large acrylic window charm for
   watch face
2 antique brass round brads
Antique brass metal spiral
2½ inches ⅜-inch-wide brown
   grosgrain ribbon
Punches: ¹⁄₁₆-inch hole, 1¾-inch circle
Die-cutting machine with postage die
Paper adhesive

clock face; attach brad for watch stem. Stamp "magic moments" along bottom of rectangle with black dye ink. Adhere assembled rectangle to right front flap.

8 Attach metal spiral to upper left corner of right front flap with a brad; tie ribbon onto clip. Trim ribbon ends at an angle. ✳

Sources: Card stock, paper pack, stamp sets, acrylic blocks, dye ink pads, acrylic window, brads, metal spiral and ribbon from Close To My Heart; distress ink pad from Ranger Industries Inc.; Cuttlebug die-cutting machine and die from Provo Craft.

Happy Birthday

DESIGN BY **DIANE TUGGLE**

Materials
Card stock: yellow, white,
    light green
Pastel striped paper
Stamp sets: Friendship Word Puzzle,
    Birthday Bash
Acrylic blocks
Dye ink pads: pink, lavender, light green
Pastel buttons: 7 mini, 3 small
White waxed thread
Paper flowers: 2 small, 1 medium
White mini round brad
Punches: 1/16-inch hole, 2-inch flower
Textile Texture embossing folder
Embossing and die-cutting machine
Adhesive dots
Paper adhesive

Project note: *Use adhesive dots to adhere paper flowers and buttons.*

1 Cut an 8 x 4¼-inch piece of yellow card stock; with long side horizontal, score a vertical line 2¼ inches from left end; fold flap to the right. Center and adhere a 5½ x 3¾-inch piece of striped paper to inside right panel.

2 Cut a 7¼ x 3½-inch piece of yellow card stock; with long side horizontal, score a vertical line 3¼ inches from right end. Fold flap to the left. Adhere left flap to right side of first piece as shown. This will form a trifold card; close left flap followed by right flap.

3 Open card and stamp desired words inside. Adhere a small flower inside card; adhere a mini button to flower center.

4 Adhere a 2 x 3¾-inch piece of striped paper to left front flap. Insert a piece of thread through three small buttons; tie a knot on top of each button and trim ends. Adhere buttons to left side of left front flap. Adhere a small flower to lower right corner of left flap; adhere a mini button to flower center.

5 Adhere a 3 x 3-inch piece of striped paper to right front flap. Referring to photo, stamp a cake, cake stand, flowers on cake and candles on a 2¼ x 2⅞-inch piece of white card stock; ink edges pink. Adhere five mini flowers along bottom of cake; adhere mini buttons to flower centers. Set aside.

6 Punch two 2-inch flowers from light green card stock; run both through embossing machine. Place medium paper flower on top of one embossed flower and punch a 1/16-inch hole through flower center; insert a brad. Adhere to upper left corner of right front flap; adhere other embossed flower to reverse side aligning flower edges. Adhere birthday cake rectangle to right front flap as shown. ✶

Sources: Card stock, Paper Garden Level 2 striped paper, stamp sets, acrylic blocks, ink pads, buttons , waxed thread, brad and flower punch from Close To My Heart; Cuttlebug embossing folder and embossing and die-cutting machine from Provo Craft.

Thanks

DESIGN BY **NIKI MEINERS**

1 Wrap polka-dot mesh around stamp wheel and ink with watermark ink; roll wheel randomly over glossy card stock; heat set ink. Cover card stock with brown dye ink; wipe off excess with paper towels. Repeat process with blue, red and brown inks. Heat set ink.

2 Apply watermark ink to butterfly; stamp butterfly centered on a 4⅛ x 4⅛-inch piece of inked card stock. Emboss with brown embossing powder.

3 Cut a 12 x 6-inch piece of iridescent card stock; with long side horizontal, score and fold vertical lines 3 inches from each end, forming a 6 x 6-inch gatefold card.

4 Open front flaps and score vertical lines 1 and 1½ inches from each end; score horizontal lines on front flaps 1½ inches above bottom edge on left front panel and 1½ inches below top edge on right front panel.

5 Cut a 4½ x 4½-inch piece of red card stock; create a border by scoring lines ⅛ inch from each edge. Adhere butterfly square to red square; adhere to right front flap.

6 Open card and adhere a 4¾ x 5-inch piece of red card stock inside. Stamp "thanks" and a flourish with brown chalk ink.

7 For band, cut a 12 x 1-inch strip of red card stock; score vertical lines 3 inches from each end. Cut an additional 1 x 1-inch square from red card stock; adhere to end of strip to extend band around card.

Materials

12 x 12-inch card stock: white glossy, dark brown iridescent, red
Chipboard flourish
Clear stamp wheel
Polka-dot mesh
Stamp sets: It's the Little Things, Sentiments O'Simple, Lifetime of Inspiration
Ink pads: watermark, brown dye, blue dye, red dye, brown chalk
Brown embossing powder
Dark red silk flower
Ivory button
Embossing heat tool
Fabric glue

8 Adhere button to flower center; adhere flower over glued section of band. Stamp "thanks" next to flower with brown chalk ink. Apply brown dye ink to chipboard flourish and adhere below "thanks." Slide band onto card. ✳

Sources: Card stock from Bazzill Basics Paper Inc.; stamp sets from Unity Stamp Co.; chalk and dye ink pads and stamp wheel from Clearsnap Inc.; chipboard shapes from Ranger Industries Inc.; flower from Prima Marketing Inc.; Fabri-Tac Glue from Beacon Adhesives Inc.

Matchbook Gift Holder

DESIGN BY **SANDRA GRAHAM SMITH**

Materials
Card stock: gold, dark green, brown
Leaves printed paper
White paper
Apple cider packet
Black fine-tip marker
6 inches ⅜-inch-wide burgundy decorative ribbon
Die-cutting machine and leaf die
⅛-inch hole punch
Paper adhesive
Computer and printer (optional)

1 Cut a 4 x 11-inch piece of gold card stock. With short side horizontal, score horizontal lines 4¾ inches and 10 inches above bottom edge. Fold up bottom flap. Adhere a 3½ x 4¾-inch piece of printed paper to center of bottom flap.

2 Place cider packet inside holder, aligning top edge with 10-inch score line; fold top 1-inch flap down. Punch two ⅛-inch holes through flap going through all layers. Insert ribbon ends through holes from front to back; cross ribbon ends over each other and insert through opposite holes back to front. Trim ribbon ends at an angle.

3 Hand-print, or use a computer to generate, the following on white paper:

"Enjoy a cup of Hot Cider—Sip and think of days to come they'll be filled with lots of fun…Getting together with friends too, and like this warming thru and thru."

4 Cut a rectangle around words; adhere to gold card stock and trim a small border. Adhere to front of holder.

5 Die-cut two leaves from dark green and brown card stock; adhere to top flap as shown. ✽

Sources: Card stock from Bazzill Basics Paper Inc.; printed paper from STARfish and Dreams; die-cutting machine and die from Sizzix.

Enjoy a cup of **Hot Cider -** Sip and think of days to come they'll be filled with lots of fun...Getting together with friends too, and like this warming thru and thru.

Celebrate

DESIGN BY **LISA SILVER**

1 Cut the following: 12 x 4¼-inch pink card stock (wallet base), 10 x 4-inch Rain Boots paper (wallet lining) and a 10 x 2-inch pink card stock (wallet pockets).

2 With long side of wallet base horizontal, score vertical lines 2 and 7 inches from left end. Score a vertical line in wallet lining and wallet pockets at 5 inches. Round top corners of wallet pockets and pierce holes along top and side edges; connect holes with gel pen to create faux stitching.

3 With pink floral side faceup, adhere wallet lining to wallet base aligning fold lines. **Note:** *Do not adhere lining to 2-inch section at left end of wallet base.* Apply adhesive along bottom, sides and fold line of wallet pockets; adhere to bottom of wallet base, aligning fold lines. **Note:** *The center areas of pockets should be left free of adhesive.*

4 Round left corners of wallet base. Pierce holes along top, left and bottom edges on front of left flap; connect holes with gel pen. Adhere a 4¾ x 4-inch piece of Patio Umbrella paper to right front flap; stamp "{celebrate}" on lower right corner with black ink.

5 For inside, cut a 4 x 3¼-inch piece of cream card stock; round corners. Stamp "Wishing you a happy

Materials

Card stock: pink, cream
Daydream printed papers: Patio Umbrella, Rain Boots
Stamp sets: Hugs and Kisses, Birthday Centers
Ink pads: black dye, pink distress
White gel pen
Pink colored pencil
Pink button
Brown waxed thread
Magnetic closure
Paper piercing tool
Corner rounder
Instant-dry paper glue

cake 'n candle day!" on rectangle with black ink; stamp hearts beside words with pink ink. Color with colored pencil. Insert inside a pocket.

6 Adhere one half of magnetic closure to center edge on back of left flap; adhere other half to right front panel so it aligns with first half. Insert thread through button; tie a knot on top and trim thread ends. Adhere button to left flap. ✱

Sources: Card stock from Prism Papers; printed papers from October Afternoon; stamp sets from Cornish Heritage Farms; distress ink pad from Ranger Industries Inc.; waxed thread from Scrapworks; Zip Dry Paper Glue from Beacon Adhesives Inc.

His & Her Gift Cards

DESIGNS BY **MELONY BRADLEY**

Materials
Card stock: kraft, dark brown
Double-sided printed papers
Rubber stamps: fern leaf, birthday
   sentiment
Ink pads: black pigment, brown dye
Silk flowers: 1 large, 1 small
⅜-inch-wide ribbon: 8 inches brown
   gingham, 3 inches "celebrate," scrap
   pieces of various colors to match
   flowers
Clear flat-back crystal
Pearl-tipped stick pin
Brads: 2 brown, 1 blue fabric-covered
Magnet strips
Punches: 2½-inch scallop circle, 2-inch
   circle, 1/16-inch hole
Circle template and cutting tool
   (optional)
¼-inch-wide double-sided tape
Instant-dry paper glue

For both cards, cut a 3½ x 11-inch piece of double-sided paper. With long side horizontal, score vertical lines 4½ and 9 inches from left end. Trim a curve at right end, using a circle template and cutting tool if desired. Fold piece to form a 3½ x 4½-inch top-flap card. Ink edges if desired.

1 Cut a 3 x 3½-inch piece of double-sided paper. Apply double-sided tape to reverse side on bottom, left and right sides; adhere inside card, leaving top edge open to create a pocket.

For His card, punch a 2½-inch scallop circle from dark brown card stock; punch a 2-inch circle from kraft card stock. Stamp a fern leaf centered on kraft circle with black ink; ink edges brown. Adhere to scallop circle. Adhere to top flap as shown.

2 Stamp a birthday sentiment centered on a 2¾ x ¾-inch piece of kraft card stock with black ink; ink edges brown. Adhere to dark brown card stock; trim a small border. Punch a ¹⁄₁₆-inch hole through each end and insert brown brads. Adhere to center bottom of card front.

3 Wrap gingham ribbon around top flap and tie a knot; trim ribbon ends as desired. Adhere one half of a magnet to reverse side of bottom of scallop circle;

adhere other half of magnet to front panel so both pieces align.

For Her card, cut a 3 x 4⅛-inch piece of printed paper and adhere to bottom front panel. Layer flowers and insert fabric-covered brad through center. Adhere to center bottom of top flap.

1 Tie scrap pieces of ribbons around stick pin; trim ends as desired. Cut "celebrate" from ribbon and wrap around top of pin; adhere to secure. Trim ends in V-notches. Insert pin through flowers. Adhere crystal to fabric brad. **Note:** *If desired, sandwich end of pin on back of top flap between two small pieces of card stock.*

2 Adhere magnet strips to card in the same manner as for His card. ✱

Sources: Printed papers and fabric-covered brad from K&Company; rubber stamps from Anna Griffin Inc. and Plaid Enterprises Inc.; "celebrate" ribbon from Making Memories; circle punches from Uchida of America; Coluzzle circle template and cutting tool from Provo Craft; Zip Dry Paper Glue from Beacon Adhesives Inc.

Materials
Pink card stock
Printed papers: black polka-dots,
    ballerina tutus, dance-themed words
White paper
Black fine-tip marker
9½ inches ⅛-inch-wide pink satin ribbon
Gold heart button
Small piece of hook-and-loop tape
⅛-inch hole punch
Adhesive foam tape
Tape
Paper adhesive
Computer and printer (optional)

1 Adhere a 6 x 3-inch piece of black polka-dot paper to a 6 x 3-inch piece of pink card stock. Use patterns on page 46 to cut a purse from a folded sheet of pink card stock and a purse flap from black/pink paper. Fold purse flap in half along dashed line; punch ⅛-inch holes on flap as indicated on pattern.

2 Insert ends of ribbon through holes and secure inside with tape. Place flap over top of purse; adhere back half of flap to back of purse. Attach one half of hook-and-loop tape to center top of purse front; attach other half to flap so it aligns with first half. Adhere button to center front of flap.

3 Adhere a 5½ x 1½-inch strip of dance-themed words paper to front of purse ⅝ inch above bottom edge; trim edges even. Cut one ballerina tutu from printed paper; adhere to pink card stock. Cut out. Adhere to right side of purse as shown with foam tape.

4 Hand-print, or use a computer to generate, "GOOD LUCK ON YOUR DANCE RECITAL" on white paper. Cut a rectangle around words and adhere inside purse. ✱

Sources: Printed papers from Karen Foster Design, Creative Imaginations and Making Memories.

PATTERNS ON PAGE 46

It's a Dance Thing

DESIGN BY **SANDRA GRAHAM SMITH**

Stars & Stripes

DESIGN BY **SANDRA GRAHAM SMITH**

1 Cut a 12 x 5½-inch piece of printed paper. With long side horizontal, score vertical lines 4¼, 8½ and 10¼ inches from left end. Cut off ¾ inch from right end using decorative-edge scissors. Beginning from left end, fold left flap to the right; fold next flap to the left; fold last flap to the right.

2 Use patterns on page 45 to cut a small star from printed paper, a medium star from blue card stock and a large star from white cardboard. Layer and adhere stars together. Turn star over and apply adhesive to right side only; adhere to center front of card. The right side of the star will be used to catch the side flap when card is closed.

3 Cut out "America" from printed paper and adhere to white card stock; trim a small border and adhere to upper left corner of card front at an angle with foam tape. ❋

Source: Printed paper from Creative Imaginations.

PATTERNS ON PAGE 45

Materials
Card stock: blue, white
Patriotic Borders double-sided printed
   paper
White cardboard
Decorative-edge scissors
Adhesive foam tape
Paper adhesive

Thinking of You

DESIGN BY **SUSAN COBB,** COURTESY OF HOT OFF THE PRESS

Materials
5 x 6½-inch blank card
Cardmaker's Pretty Creative Pack
Pretty Creative Kit
Fold & Stack Flowers template
Black fine-tip pen
Black dye ink pad
Awl
Mini adhesive dots
Vellum adhesive dots
Paper adhesive
Computer and printer (optional)

1 Adhere a 1 x 6½-inch strip of burgundy paper to left side of card front. Adhere a 4⅞ x 6½-inch piece of blue floral paper to card front, aligning right edges. Ink card edges.

2 For a Double Daisy flower, place template on back of burgundy paper and trace six shapes. Cut out shapes and cut side areas as indicated on template. Poke a hole through center of each with awl.

3 To assemble, fold and then unfold to create a 3-D effect. Place one piece on top of another and tuck both petals behind first layer. Add additional pieces and continue to tuck them in place. Attach together with a brad to hold petals in place. Set aside.

4 Use template to trace and cut out three Amy shapes from vellum. Cut areas at sides of shapes as indicated on template and poke a hole through center of each shape. Place together as for daisy.

5 Insert a dark pink mini brad at center of a light green silk flower and then place brad through center of vellum flower. Remove brad from burgundy flower and attach silk and vellum flowers to center of burgundy flower. Attach to upper right area of card front with a mini adhesive dot.

6 Hand-print, or use a computer to generate, "Thinking of you" on light green tag. Ink edges and attach a dark pink mini brad to left end. Adhere to lower right area of card front.

7 For inside, ink edges of a 5 x 2½-inch piece of blue floral paper; adhere inside card. Hand-print, or use a computer to generate, "On this beautiful day" on vellum; cut out and adhere to burgundy paper with vellum dots; trim a small border. Adhere to blue floral rectangle, aligning right edges. Attach a dark pink mini brad through center of a light green silk flower and adhere to upper left corner of vellum rectangle. ✹

Source: Creative Pack, Creative Kit and template from Hot Off The Press.

Friendship Blooms

DESIGN BY **TESSA BUNDY**,
COURTESY OF HOT OFF THE PRESS

1 Adhere yellow words paper to card front; trim edges even. With card fold at top, adhere a 6½ x 2-inch piece of light green paper to bottom of card front. Ink edges of card.

2 Use template to trace five roses on back of pink paper; cut out and draw stitching around edges with black pen. Fold petals inward along fold lines working clockwise. Attach a yellow brad to center of each rose. Attach four roses across card front as shown with foam tape.

3 Use template to trace five flower stems on back of yellow words paper. **Note:** *Draw three stems with template faceup; draw two stems with template facedown.* Cut out stems and ink edges. Adhere a stem beneath each rose on card front; trim edges even.

4 Hand-print, or use a computer to generate, "FRIEND" on a 4⅛ x ¾-inch piece of light green paper; draw stitching along edges. Adhere to pink

Materials

6½ x 5-inch blank card
Cardmaker's Citrus Creative Pack
Citrus Creative Kit
Fold-It Swirls template
Black dye ink pad
Black fine-tip pen
Craft knife
Adhesive foam tape
Paper adhesive
Computer and printer (optional)

paper; trim a narrow border. Ink edges. Adhere to center top of card with foam tape.

5 For inside, cut a 4 x 1½-inch rectangle from yellow words paper; draw stitching around edges. Adhere inside card to upper right area. Cut a 5 x 2-inch rectangle from light green paper; draw stitching around edges. Hand-print desired message on right side of light green rectangle, leaving some space on left side. Adhere inside card, overlapping yellow rectangle. Use foam tape to adhere remaining rose and flower stem to left side of light green rectangle. ✻

Source: Creative Pack, Creative Kit and template from Hot Off The Press.

Giant Thank You

DESIGN BY **TESSA BUNDY,** COURTESY OF HOT OFF THE PRESS

Materials
Floral Backgrounds printed papers
Giant Fold-It Flower Card template
Brown brads: 1 large, 4 mini
Brown dye ink pad
Fine-tip pens: brown, black
¾-inch circle punch
Craft knife
Paper adhesive

1 With reverse sides facing, adhere a sheet of brown floral paper to a sheet of pink printed paper. Flip template and trace flower on pink printed side. Cut out and crease each petal upward along inner fold lines. Crease each petal back along outer fold lines. Open and ink edges of petals and folded outer sections. With pink printed side faceup, use flipped template to trace swirls on each small outer petal. Go over swirls with brown pen.

2 Use template to trace five tags on cream paper. Cut out and ink edges. Use black pen to hand-write "Thank You" on one tag; write desired messages on remaining tags. Attach a mini brad to each message tag. **Note:** *Do not attach a brad to "Thank You" tag.*

With pink printed side faceup, adhere the four message tags in pairs to left and right-most petals as shown.

3 Use template to trace additional swirls onto remaining petals as desired. Close card, folding back outer sections and then working counterclockwise to fold in large petals. Untuck edges of inner flaps if they have overlapped.

4 Use craft knife to cut a hole at center of giant flower; attach large brad through top of "Thank You" tag and then through center of flower. Lift brad gently while folding back prongs so there is enough room beneath to easily slip petals in and out. Punch a ¾-inch circle from brown floral paper; ink edges and adhere to top of large brad. ✻

Source: Printed papers, brads and template from Hot Off The Press.

Star Birthday

DESIGN BY **SUSAN COBB,** COURTESY OF HOT OFF THE PRESS

1 Position template on back of a sheet of striped paper; trace outline and fold lines. Remove template and cut around outer edges of star.

2 Ink edges on striped side. Fold each point inward on inner fold line and then unfold; fold each outer area inward along fold line and unfold. Working clockwise, fold large points inward. After first fold, you will need to tuck the next fold under the previous one. Repeat tucking with each fold.

3 Use template to create a mini star from burgundy dotted paper; ink edges. Attach mini star to center of star card with a green brad.

4 Hand-write, or use a computer to generate, "Happy Birthday" on a small tag and "Have a special day!" on a label. Adhere label centered inside card. Attach a green brad to small tag and adhere to outside of card as shown. ✳

Source: Papers, brads and template from Hot Off The Press.

Materials
Autumn Backgrounds papers
Giant Star Card template
Autumn brads pack
Black fine-tip pen
Brown dye ink pad
Craft knife
Paper adhesive
Computer and printer (optional)

A Dress for All Occasions

DESIGN BY **DONNA MALIGNO**

Materials
Card stock: light green,
    green, white
Light green floral printed paper
Dots rubber stamp
Light green distress ink pad
White pearlescent dimensional paint
1½ inches ⅛-inch-wide white
    satin ribbon
Oval scallop punches: medium,
    large, mega
Small flower punch
Distressing tool
Paper adhesive

1 Form a 4¼ x 5½-inch side-folded card from light green card stock. Cut a 3¾ x 4¾-inch rectangle from printed paper and a 4 x 5-inch rectangle from

white card stock. Distress edges of white rectangle. Adhere rectangles together and center and adhere to card front.

2 Punch the following from printed paper: two medium ovals, one large oval and one mega oval. Fold one oval in half with printed side as the outside (Fig. 1). With straight edge at top, fold sides downward until they meet in the center (Figs. 2 and 3). Repeat for each oval. Fold second medium oval so only four scallops are showing along curved edge; this will be the top of the dress. Fold back scalloped edge of mega oval back behind front scalloped edge, forming a straight line (Fig. 4).

3 Stamp dots randomly on a 2½ x 3-inch piece of white card stock. Adhere to a 2¾ x 3¼-inch piece of light green card stock. Distress edges.

4 Referring to photo, arrange and adhere folded ovals to stamped rectangle to form a dress. Tie a knot at center of ribbon; arrange and adhere to waist of dress. Center and adhere assembled rectangle to card front.

5 Punch five flowers from green card stock and three flowers from printed paper. Layer and adhere flowers to upper left and lower right corners of center rectangle. Accent flower centers and scallops on dress with paint; let dry. ✽

Sources: Card stock from Bazzill Basics Paper Inc.; rubber stamp from Stamps by Judith; distress ink pad from Ranger Industries Inc.; pearlescent paint from Duncan Enterprises; punches from Uchida of America.

PATTERNS ON PAGE 45

Bridal Dress

DESIGN BY **DONNA MALIGNO**

1 Form a 4¼ x 5½-inch side-folded card from white card stock. Stamp a flourish in each corner of a 3½ x 4½-inch piece of white card stock; center and adhere to a 4 x 5¼-inch piece of pink card stock. Center and adhere to card front. Use oval template to cut a 2¾ x 3½-inch oval from pink printed paper; center and adhere to card front.

2 Punch the following from white text weight paper: two medium ovals, one large oval and one mega oval. Follow instructions from A Dress for All Occasions card to tea bag fold ovals to form a dress. Arrange and adhere folded ovals to pink oval on card front.

3 Stamp "Best Wishes" on a scrap piece of white card stock; trim with decorative-edge scissors. Ink edges. Adhere to lower right corner of card front with foam tape.

4 Punch two ⅛-inch holes through left side of card front approximately ¾ inch apart. Thread ribbon through holes and a tie a bow on outside of card; trim ribbon ends in V-notches.

5 Punch three tiny flowers and one daisy from white text weight paper; cut daisy apart to form small leaves. Color with markers. Adhere one flower to right side of waist on dress; adhere other two flowers and leaves to center top of pink oval. Accent dress and oval with glitter glue; let dry. ✳

Sources: Card stock from Bazzill Basics Paper Inc.; flourish stamp from Inkadinkado; chalk ink pad from Clearsnap Inc.; oval tempalte from Creative Memories; scallop oval punches from Uchida of America; glitter glue from Ranger Industries Inc.

Materials

Card stock: white, pink
White text weight paper
Pink printed paper
Stamps: flourish, "Best Wishes"
Pink chalk ink pad
Markers: pink, green
12 inches ½-inch-wide white organdy ribbon
Scallop oval punches: medium, large, mega
Punches: tiny flower, small daisy, ⅛-inch hole
Oval template
Decorative-edge scissors
White glitter glue
Adhesive foam tape
Paper adhesive

A Day at the Beach

DESIGN BY **DONNA MALIGNO**

1 Form a 4¼ x 4¼-inch top-folded card from yellow card stock. Cut a 4 x 4-inch piece of white card stock. Lay a piece of scrap paper across white square approximately two-thirds the way down. Use felt pad to apply distress inks across lower portion of square to form the appearance of water. Accent water with glitter glue; let dry.

2 Tear a small piece of scrap paper into the shape of a cloud. Randomly place torn piece on top half of square and stipple blue ink around edges. Repeat to form several clouds.

3 Cut one 4 x 1-inch strip and one 4 x 1¼-inch strip of sandpaper; tear off top of each piece. Layer and adhere to bottom of square, leaving center top of top strip free of adhesive.

4 Cut five 1¾ x 1¾-inch squares from printed paper. With printed side as the outside, fold one square in half diagonally (Fig. 1). Unfold and fold in half diagonally again in opposite direction, forming a triangle with crease down the middle (Figs. 2 and 3). Fold right and left flaps down to center fold (Figs. 4 and 5). Repeat for each square.

5 Turn folded shapes over. Adhere two shapes together (Fig. 6). Continue to adhere shapes in the same manner until all shapes are connected.

Materials
Card stock: yellow, white, dark green
Yellow printed paper
Scrap paper
Distress ink pads: blue, light green
Green pearlescent dimensional paint
6 inches ⅜-inch-wide green satin ribbon
Stippling brush
Felt pad
Sandpaper
Clear glitter glue
Paper adhesive

6 Cut a ³⁄₁₆ x 2-inch strip of dark green card stock. Tuck end of strip behind center top of sandpaper strip and adhere. Adhere side flaps of assembled umbrella to card front as shown. ***Note:*** *Do not adhere center area of umbrella. This will pop up and be dimensional.* Accent umbrella with paint; let dry. Tie a bow with ribbon; trim ribbon ends at an angle and adhere to umbrella stand as shown. ✳

Sources: Card stock from Bazzill Basics Paper Inc.; pearlescent paint, distress ink pads , foam pad and glitter glue from Ranger Industries Inc.

PATTERNS ON PAGE 45

Stars & Stripes
CONTINUED FROM PAGE 37

A Dress for All Occasions
CONTINUED FROM PAGE 42

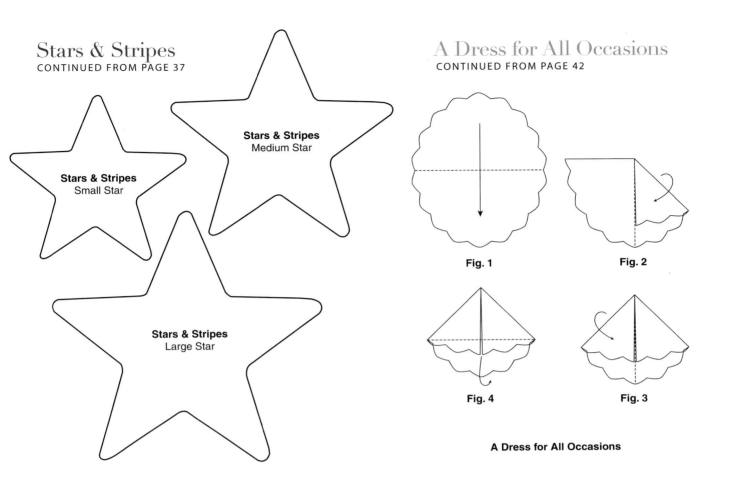

Stars & Stripes
Small Star

Stars & Stripes
Medium Star

Stars & Stripes
Large Star

Fig. 1

Fig. 2

Fig. 4

Fig. 3

A Dress for All Occasions

A Day at the Beach
CONTINUED FROM PAGE 44

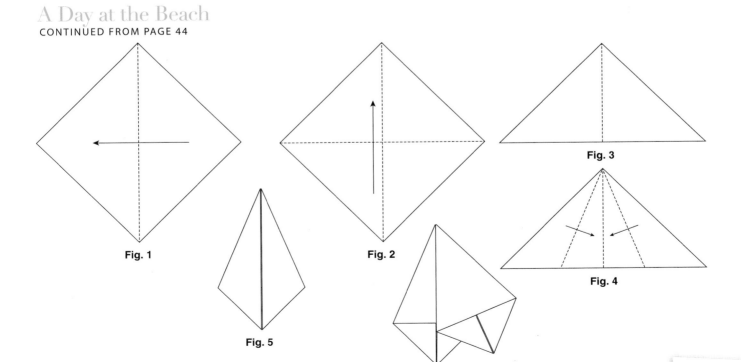

Fig. 1

Fig. 2

Fig. 3

Fig. 4

Fig. 5

Fig. 6

A Day at the Beach

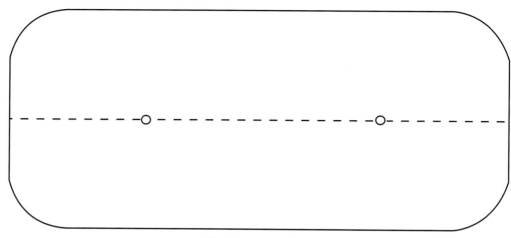

It's a Dance Thing
Purse Flap
Score and fold on dashed line

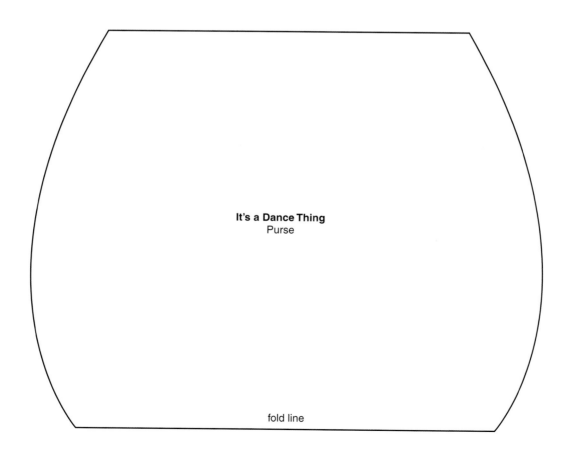

It's a Dance Thing
Purse

fold line

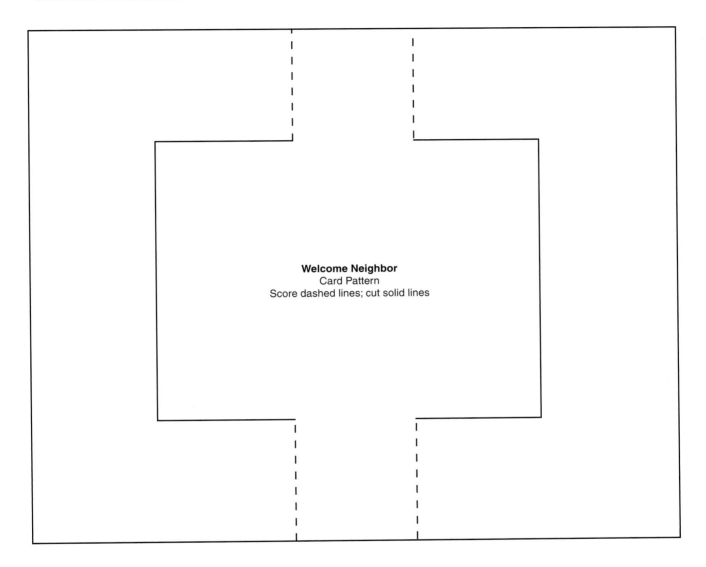

Welcome Neighbor
Card Pattern
Score dashed lines; cut solid lines

Buyer's Guide

The Buyer's Guide listings are provided as a service to our readers and should not be considered an endorsement from this publication.

American Crafts Inc.
(801) 226-0747
www.americancrafts.com

Anna Griffin Inc.
(888) 817-8170
www.annagriffin.com

Autumn Leaves
(800) 727-2727
www.creativityinc.com

BasicGrey
(801) 544-1116
www.basicgrey.com

Bazzill Basics Paper Inc.
(800) 560-1610
www.bazzillbasics.com

Beacon Adhesives Inc.
(914) 699-3405
www.beaconcreates.com

Best Creation Inc.
www.bestcreation.us

Chatterbox Inc.
(877) 749-7797
www.chatterboxinc.com

Clearsnap Inc.
(888) 448-4862
www.clearsnap.com

Close To My Heart
(888) 655-6552
www.closetomyheart.com

Colorbök
www.colorbok.com

Cornish Heritage Farms
(877) 860-5328
www.cornishheritagefarms.com

Creative Imaginations
(800) 942-6487
www.creativeimaginations.us

Creative Memories
(800) 468-9335
www.creativememories.com

Doodlebug Design Inc.
(877) 800-9190
www.doodlebug.ws

EK Success
www.eksuccess.com

Fiskars
(866) 348-5661
www.fiskarscrafts.com

Frances Meyer Inc.
(413) 584-5446
www.francesmeyer.com

Hot Off The Press
(888) 300-3406
www.paperwishes.com

K&Company
(888) 244-2083
www.kandcompany.com

Kaisercraft
(888) 684-7147
www.kaisercraft.net/site

Karen Foster Design
(801) 451-9779
www.karenfosterdesign.com

Making Memories
(800) 286-5263
www.makingmemories.com

McGill Inc.
(800) 286-5263
www.mcgillinc.com

Memory Box
www.memoryboxco.com

My Mind's Eye
(800) 665-5116
www.mymindseye.com

October Afternoon
(866) 513-5553
www.octoberafternoon.com

Plaid Enterprises Inc.
(800) 842-4197
www.plaidonline.com

Prima Marketing Inc.
(909) 627-5532
www.primamarketinginc.com

Prism Papers
(866) 902-1002
www.prismpapers.com

Provo Craft
(800) 937-7686
www.provocraft.com

Ranger Industries Inc.
(732) 389-3535
www.rangerink.com

The Ribbons House
(787) 793-6201
www.ribbonshouse.wordpress.com

Scenic Route Paper Co.
(801) 542-8071
www.scenicroutepaper.com

Scrapworks
(801) 363-1010
www.scrapworks.com

Sizzix
(877) 355-4766
www.sizzix.com

Stampabilities
(800) 888-0321
www.stampabilities.com

Stampin' Up!
(800) STAMP UP (782-6787)
www.stampinup.com

STARfish & Dreams
(888) 6STARFISH (678-2734)
www.starfishanddreams.com

Technique Tuesday
(503) 644-4073
www.techniquetuesday.com

Uchida of America
(800) 541-5877
www.marvy.com

Unity Stamp Co.
(877) 862-2329
www.unitystampco.com

We R Memory Keepers
(877) 742-5937
www.weronthenet.com

WorldWin Papers
(888) 843-6455
www.worldwinpapers.com